W9-AAE-016

az HUMANITIES
EXPLORE. SHARE. EXPERIENCE.

1242 N. Central Ave.
Phoenix, AZ 85004

mother earth's lullaby

A Song for Endangered Animals

Written by **Terry Pierce**

Illustrated by **Carol Heyer**

TILBURY HOUSE PUBLISHERS, THOMASTON, MAINE

3 1740 12523 2110

When Mother Earth bids goodnight,
she casts her shafts of silver light.
She says, "Goodnight, my precious ones."
Nature's song has just begun.

Bamboo leaves flutter–flap.
Panda cub curls up to nap.

Wallaby—off he goes,
hops inside where he can doze.

Underneath the stars aglow,
condors hear the waves below.

Newborn cubs are warm within
Mama's silent snowy den.

Now to rest, sleepy one.

Slumber calls, day is done.

Darkness is a gift for you.

Hear the red wolf howl, "Ow—oooo."

Tiger kits rumble-purr,
tucked against their mother's fur.

Toucan brood, in a tree,
hear the jungle's melody.

Rhino calf falls asleep,
cozy in a rumpled heap.

Dolphins swimming in the sea,
rest side by side in harmony.

Now to rest, sleepy one.

Slumber calls, day is done.

Darkness is a gift for you.

Hear the owl call out, "Who-hoooo."

Nēnē young quieting,
get warm below their mama's wing.

Snuggle down, drowsy fawn,
swaddled in your bed till dawn.

Mother Earth has bid goodnight,
and swathed the world in silver light.
Everyone feels safe and snug,
all wrapped up in nature's hug.

Giant panda

Giant pandas live in the bamboo forests of central China. They spend half their wakeful time eating, mostly bamboo leaves. Habitat loss from human activity and development endangered pandas for decades. Thanks to efforts to preserve their natural homes, however, panda populations have risen in recent years.

Yellow-footed rock wallaby

These wallabies live in the vast, sparsely populated interior of Australia, the region known as the Outback. As more humans have settled in the Outback, the rock wallaby's numbers have dropped. Livestock (goats) and predators (foxes, cats) introduced by settlers now threaten the wallaby's status.

California condor

Condors soar over the coastal mountains of California and Grand Canyon National Park in Arizona. Their ten-foot wingspan is wider than two ten-year-old children lying head-to-toe! Fewer than 150 live in the wild. Human activities (hunting, powerlines, pollution, and trash accidentally eaten by condors) threaten these critically endangered birds.

Polar bear

Female polar bears dig deeply into snowdrifts for protection from the Arctic's harsh elements. They usually give birth to twins, who stay with their mother for a little over two years. Polar bears use sea ice to travel, hunt, and raise their cubs. Rising temperatures caused by climate change are melting their icy habitat and threatening their way of life.

American red wolf

Red wolves once roamed throughout the southeastern U.S. In 1980, on the brink of extinction due to hunting and habitat loss, they were bred in captivity by animal conservationists and re-introduced to the wild. North Carolina is the only remaining home to red wolves, with only about 100 left.

Sumatran tiger

These natives of Indonesia are the smallest of all tigers but still weigh more than 200 pounds when fully grown, which is more than the average grown man! Their biggest threats are illegal hunting (called poaching) and habitat loss due to deforestation as people cut down forests to sell the lumber.

Javan rhinoceros

These small rhinoceroses now live only on the island of Java in Indonesia. Unlike their African cousins, these rhinos have a single horn on their snout. Some people believe the horn has special healing powers, which has led to overhunting and declining numbers. Additionally, deforestation has shrunk their natural habitat, making them even more threatened.

Red-tailed Amazon parrot

These colorful parrots are confined to small areas in southeastern Brazil, where they nest in mangrove trees and coastal forests. Their vibrant colors make them attractive in the illegal wild bird market, to be caught and sold as pets. There is good news, however, as efforts to help the parrots through educational programs and creating sanctuaries have helped their numbers rise in recent years.

Vaquita dolphin

Vaquitas live in the northern coastal waters of the Gulf of California. Fishermen legally and illegally harvest fish, shrimp, and squid from these rich waters. Nets used to catch seafood accidentally catch vaquita, including large gillnets used to illegally catch another endangered animal, the totoaba fish. Fewer than thirty vaquita remain in the wild, making them

Northern spotted owl

These well-camouflaged small owls live exclusively in the old-growth forests of the Pacific Northwest. Habitat loss from over-logging and land development are their biggest threats. In recent years, conservationists have worked toward more effective management of the old-growth forests.

Hawaiian goose

Nēnē (pronounced: *nay-nay*) live on the Hawaiian Islands. They nest on the ground in the grasslands, scrublands, and lava flows. The challenges they face are the growing numbers of human-introduced predators (such as mongoose, cats, and dogs) and loss of their natural habitat.

Key deer

Key deer live only in the Florida Keys. They stand about two feet high at the shoulder, making them the smallest deer in North America. Once, poaching and habitat loss reduced their population to fewer than fifty, but the creation of the National Key Deer Refuge has given the tiny deer a place to recover their numbers.

Endangered Animals Can Recover!

Fortunately, the news about Mother Earth's endangered animals isn't all bad. Around the globe, on land, sea, and air, conservation efforts are paying off. Here are a few success stories.

The Indian rhino has charged back! At one point fewer than 200 of them roamed the grasslands and savannas of northern India and Nepal. But after decades of strict protection by Nepalese and Indian wildlife authorities, their numbers have grown to over 3,500.

At the Archie Carr National Wildlife Refuge in Florida, green sea turtles have swum back from the brink. Three decades ago, only 50 nests occupied the 20-mile stretch of beach, but thanks to conservation efforts, researchers tallied over 12,000 nests in 2015. While sea turtles throughout the world still face serious threats, Florida's green sea turtle recovery gives hope for sea turtle recovery in other places too.

Sound the trumpets! Trumpeter swans dominated the Great Lakes region of the U.S. a hundred years ago, but by the 1930s they were on the verge of extinction from overhunting for food. Now, thanks to the efforts of multiple state and federal wildlife management authorities, trumpeter swan numbers have flown sky high with an estimated 17,000 birds.

The eagles have landed! The bald eagle, the national bird of the United States, had an estimated population of more than 300,000 in the 1700s, but by the 1950s there were only 412 nesting pairs left in the United States excluding Alaska. Overhunting, poaching, habitat loss, powerline electrocutions, and the pesticide DDT had almost wiped them out. But eagles have since made a dramatic recovery thanks to legal protections and the banning of DDT in 1972. Now they nest throughout the U.S. and Canada, and their numbers are soaring toward what they were 300 years ago.

To learn about how you can help threatened or endangered animals, please visit:
Endangered Species Coalition: *10 Easy Things You Can Do to Save Endangered Species.*
http://www.endangered.org/10-easy-things-you-can-do-to-save-endangered-species/

TERRY PIERCE was a Montessori teacher for 22 years before writing children's books. Her 22 books include *Tae Kwon Do!* (Bank Street College Best Children's Books of 2007); *Mama Loves You So; Blackberry Banquet; Mother Goose Rhymes* (a 2007 AEP Distinguished Achievement Award Winner) and *My Busy Green Garden*. She serves on the board of the educational nonprofit organization Whaletimes, Inc., and is an instructor in the UCLA Extension Writers' Program.

CAROL HEYER has illustrated 32 children's picture books including *Humphrey's First Christmas* and *Once Upon a Cool Motorcycle Dude*, winner of eight state awards, as well as several Hank Zipzer books written by Henry Winkler. Formerly she was a production designer and writer of feature films including *Thunder Run* (1986), and she illustrated game materials for *Dungeons & Dragons* and the collectible card game *Magic: The Gathering*. Her art is included in the collections of the Greisinger Middle Earth Museum in Switzerland and the Mazza Museum, the world's largest museum of original artwork by children's book illustrators, and has won awards from The Society of Children's Book Writers and Illustrators, Spectrum, The International Competition for Fantastic Art, The Carnegie Art Institute, and The Society of Illustrators LA, among others. She is shown here with her dogs Cashew Nut and Peanut.

Tilbury House Publishers
12 Starr Street
Thomaston, Maine 04861
800-582-1899 • www.tilburyhouse.com

Text © 2018 by Terry Pierce
Illustrations © 2018 by Carol Heyer

Hardcover ISBN 978-0-88448-557-5
eBook ISBN 978-0-88448-559-9

First hardcover printing September 2018

15 16 17 18 19 20 XXX 10 9 8 7 6 5 4 3 2 1

All rights reserved. No part of this publication may be reproduced or transmitted in any
form or by any means, electronic or mechanical, including photocopying, recording, or any
information storage or retrieval system, without permission in writing from the publisher.

Library of Congress Control Number: 2018944807

Designed by Frame25 Productions
Printed in China through Four Colour Print Group

Tilbury House Nature Books seek to combine scientific accuracy
with storytelling magic. If you like this book, you'll also enjoy:

My Busy Green Garden

978-0-88448-495-0

by Terry Pierce, illustrated
by Carol Schwartz

**The World
Never Sleeps**

978-0-88448-561-2

by Natalie Rompella,
illustrated by Carol Schwartz

**Before We Eat:
From Farm to Table**

978-0-88448-652-7

by Pat Brisson, illustrated
by Mary Azarian

**The Eye of the Whale:
A Rescue Story**

978-0-88448-395-3

by Jennifer O'Connell

and other picture books at www.tilburyhouse.com